Food around the world

China

Polly Goodman

WAYLAND

First published in Great Britain in 2006 by Wayland,
a division of Hachette Children's Books, an Hachette
UK Company

Copyright © 2006 Wayland

This paperback edition published in 2010 by Wayland

Reprinted in 2010 by Wayland

Hachette Children's Books
338 Euston Road, London NW1 3BH
www.hachette.co.uk

Editor: Sarah Gay
Senior Design Manager: Rosamund Saunders
Designer: Tim Mayer
Consultant: Susannah Blake

British Library Cataloguing in Publication Data
Goodman, Polly
    China. - (Food around the world)
    1.Food habits - China - Juvenile literature 2.Cookery,
    Chinese - Juvenile literature 3.China - Social life and
    customs - Juvenile literature
    I.Title
    394.1'2'0951

ISBN 978-0-7502-6173-9

Cover photograph: street vendors at a colourful
market in Beijing.

Photo credits: Jose Fuste Raga/Corbis 6, Nevada
Wier/CORBIS 8, Wayland Picture Library 9, 16 and 17,
Andrew Sydenham/Anthony Blake Photo Library 10,
Keren Su/Lonely Planet 11, Martin Brigdale/Anthony
Blake Photo Library 12, China Photos/Reuters/Corbis 13
and title page, Yann Layma/Getty Images 14, Tim
Hill/Anthony Blake Photo Library 15, Ips Co
Ltd/Photolibrary 18, Mark Henley/Panos Pictures 19,
Greg Elms/LonelyPlanet 20, Ric Ergenbright/CORBIS 21,
Richard Jones/sinopix 22, Royalty-Free/Corbis 23,
Rawdon Wyatt/Anthony Blake Photo Library 24, Oliver
Strewe/Lonely Planet 25, Eaglemoss Consumer
Publications/Anthony Blake Photo Library 26, Jon
Hicks/CORBIS cover.

The website addresses (URLs) included in this book
were valid at the time of going to press. However,
because of the nature of the Internet, it is possible that
some addresses may have changed, or sites may have
changed or closed down since publication. While the
author and publisher regret any inconvenience this may
cause the readers, no responsibility for any such changes
can be accepted by either the author or the publisher.

Contents

Words in **bold** can be found in the glossary on page 28

Welcome to China

China is the largest country in Asia. People have been cooking delicious dishes there since ancient times. Today, Chinese tea, rice and noodle dishes are popular all over the world. There are hundreds of different dishes, cooked in various ways.

▼ China has mountains, valleys, deserts, **plains**, rivers and islands.

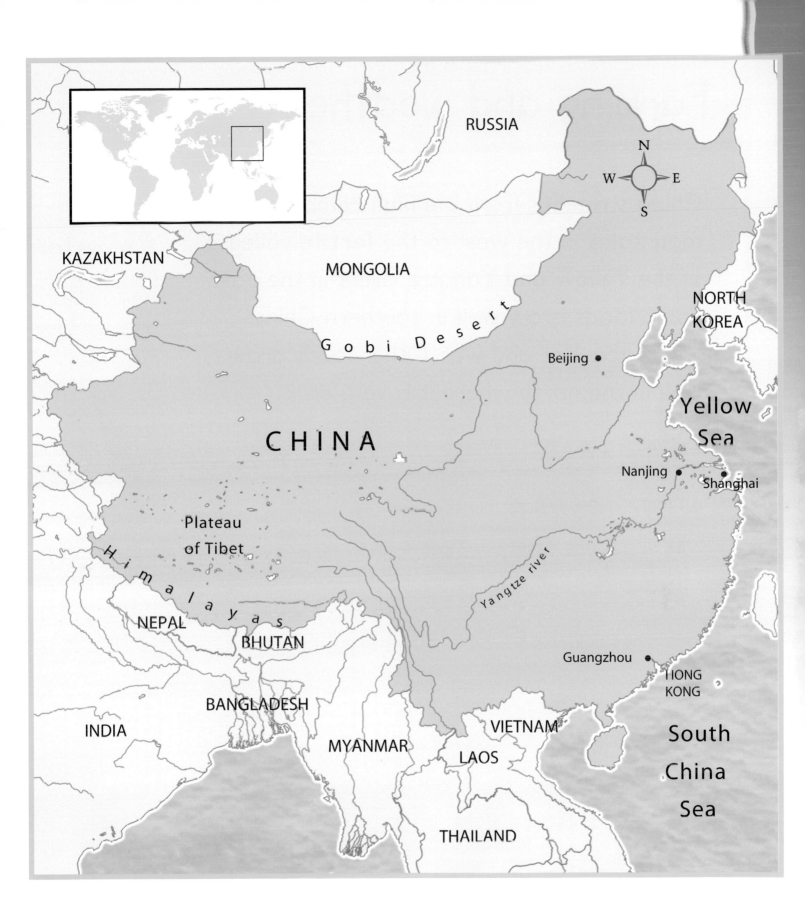

RUSSIA

N
W   E
S

KAZAKHSTAN

MONGOLIA

NORTH
KOREA

G o b i   D e s e r t

Beijing •

Yellow
Sea

CHINA

Nanjing •
Shanghai •

Plateau
of Tibet

H i m a l a y a s

Yangtze river

NEPAL

BHUTAN

Guangzhou •

HONG
KONG

BANGLADESH

INDIA

VIETNAM

South

MYANMAR

LAOS

China

Sea

THAILAND

▲ *China is marked in orange on this map. It has*
more people than any other country in the world.

Farming and weather

China stretches from the high Himalayan mountains in the west to the **fertile** valleys of the Yellow and Yangtze rivers in the east. Some foods grow well in southern China where it is hot and wet. Other foods grow well in the north where it is very dry.

▼ *Women herd sheep in the dry mountains of north-west China.*

The hot, **humid** south is ideal for growing rice. Farmers also raise pigs, chickens and ducks. In the north and west it is too dry to grow rice, so wheat and maize are grown instead. Sheep and cows graze in the hills.

▲ *Farmers use buffalo to pull ploughs through the wet rice fields.*

9

Rice and wheat

Rice is eaten with most meals in southern China. It is boiled and often fried with meat, seafood, eggs or vegetables. Rice is sometimes boiled in beef or vegetable stock to make a soup-like dish called **congee**.

▼ Rice was boiled, then fried with eggs and peas to make this dish of egg-fried rice.

Wheat flour is used to make noodles,
pancakes, steamed buns and dumplings.
Noodles are **stir-fried** or added to soups.
Pancakes and dumplings are steamed and
filled with meat or vegetables.

▲ When fresh
noodles are
made, they are
hung out in the
sun to dry.

Food fact
Chinese noodles can be made from wheat,
rice, soya beans, eggs or corn.

Vegetables, pulses and fruit

Vegetables are very important in Chinese cooking. Beansprouts, bamboo shoots, water chestnuts and mushrooms are all popular. **Pulses** are also used in many Chinese dishes. Soya beans are used to make **soy sauce** and **beancurd**.

▼ *This dish is a mixture of fried beancurd and Chinese shiitake mushrooms.*

Tropical fruits such as mango, **lychees**, **starfruit**, kiwifruit, bananas and **papaw** are grown in China. People eat them fresh or use them to make desserts and drinks.

▲ Some Chinese towns hold lychee festivals. Everybody tastes the ripe lychee fruits.

Fish and meat

China has over 2,000 kilometres of coastline where prawns, lobster, **shad** and mullet are caught. Prawns are also kept in ponds on fish farms. Perch and other freshwater fish are caught in China's rivers. Fish is usually steamed or stir-fried.

▼ Fishermen sort a large catch of fish into baskets.

◄ Crispy fried duck, spring onions and cucumber are rolled in steamed pancakes. This dish is called Peking Duck.

Pork is the most common meat in China. Chicken and duck are also popular. They are cooked slowly in stews, stir-fried or steamed.

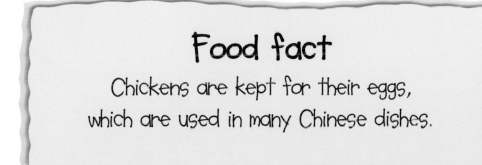

Food fact
Chickens are kept for their eggs, which are used in many Chinese dishes.

Shopping and street food

Fresh fruit, vegetables, meat and fish are sold in open markets. There are also small general stores selling rice, milk and other everyday goods. Some big towns and cities have large supermarkets.

◀ *There is an open market in every Chinese village, town and city.*

On city streets, people sell traditional Chinese food such as steamed buns and watermelon seeds, or pork and cabbage rolls called **chiaotse**. They make quick snacks or lunches for office workers.

◀ Steamed buns filled with meat and vegetables are made on a street stall.

Food fact
The Chinese love jasmine tea and green tea, which are drunk without milk or sugar.

Mealtimes in China

Everyday Chinese meals might include dishes from the menus below.

Breakfast

Rice porridge with dumplings

Doughnut with hot **soymilk**

Milk or jasmine tea

Lunch

Vegetable noodle soup

Chinese leaves with beancurd

◀ *The Chinese drink jasmine or green tea with most meals.*

Dinner

Peanut salad

Radish and carrot pickle

Red-braised pork with chestnuts

Steamed fish in lotus leaves

Stir-fried cauliflower

Red-braised mushrooms

Vegetable soup

Fresh watermelon

Fresh oranges

Jasmine or green tea

▲ The Chinese eat with chopsticks, which they hold between their thumb and their first two fingers.

Around the country

Each region of China has its own special style of cooking. In the south, rice is the most important food and **dimsum** are often eaten. Pork is the most common type of meat in the south. In the east, people eat fish, clear soups and **jiaozi** dumplings.

◀ Dimsum are steamed or fried snacks such as spring rolls, prawn dumplings or pork buns.

In western China, hot and spicy dishes are made with **Sichuan peppercorns** and chillies. In the north, wheat noodles are more common than rice. Peking duck, fried beancurd and **water chestnuts** are favourites in this region.

▲ *Noodles are often served in a soup, like this bowl of vegetable and noodle soup.*

Special occasions

On birthdays, weddings and other special occasions, people eat foods that have special meanings. Noodles are eaten at birthday parties because they stand for a long and happy life.

◄ *These birthday buns are made to look like peaches. In China, peaches stand for a long life.*

Food fact

In China, foods have different meanings. Sugar stands for a sweet life and oranges mean wealth.

Chinese weddings can last for up to four days and the highlight of each day is a feast. Red dishes are often served because red is the colour of happiness. By eating these dishes, the guests wish the bride and groom a happy marriage.

▲ *Chinese wedding cakes are baked and filled with red or green bean paste.*

23

Festival food

The biggest festival in China is the New Year Festival. In northern China, families put a coin inside one of their jiaozi dumplings. Whoever finds it is wished good luck for the new year. In the south, people eat a special sticky cake, which stands for friendships lasting.

◀ *Vegetable spring rolls look like gold bars and represent wealth in the new year.*

The Moon Festival takes place on the day of the new moon, in September or October each year. Families get together and eat round cakes with sweet centres, called moon cakes.

▼ A tray of freshly baked moon cakes is ready for the Moon Festival.

Make some Chinese soup!

What you need

- 1 tin of sweetcorn
- 2 spring onions
- 750ml chicken stock
- 170g cooked chicken, diced
- 1 tablespoon sugar

What to do

1. Slice the spring onions finely.
2. Put the sweetcorn and spring onions in a saucepan with the chicken and stock.
3. Bring to the boil and simmer with a lid on for 10 minutes.
4. Add the sugar and simmer for 5 minutes.

Ask an adult to help you make this soup. Always be careful with sharp knives and hot pans.

This food pyramid shows which foods you should eat to have a healthy, **balanced diet**.

We shouldn't eat too many fats, oils, cakes or sweets.

Milk, cheese, meat, fish, beans and eggs help to keep us strong.

We should eat plenty of vegetables and fruit to keep healthy.

Bread, cereal, rice and pasta should make up most of our diet.

Chinese meals use all foods from the pyramid. Some dishes are fried in oil, but most are made of rice or noodles with vegetables and some fish or meat, which helps to balance Chinese diets.

Glossary

balanced diet a diet that includes a mixture of different foods which supply all the things a body needs to keep healthy

beancurd a paste made from mashed soya beans

chiaotse rolls of pastry filled with pork and cabbage

congee a soup-like dish made from rice boiled in beef or vegetable stock

dimsum steamed or fried snacks such as spring rolls, prawn dumplings or pork buns

fertile land that is good for growing crops

humid moist or damp

jiaozi dumplings filled with pork mince and Chinese cabbage or other fillings

lychee a sweet, fleshy fruit with a spiny skin

papaw a fruit with an orange flesh and small black seeds

plain a large area of flat land

pulses beans, peas and other foods that are edible seeds

shad a type of fish in the herring family

Sichuan peppercorns the dried seeds of a plant grown in the Sichuan province of China, which give food a hot taste

soymilk a rich, creamy milk made from soya beans

soy sauce a sauce made from soya beans

starfruit a yellow, star-shaped fruit with a ribbed skin

stir-fried a dish that has been fried rapidly while stirring and tossing

water chestnuts the edible roots of a plant that grows in freshwater ponds, marshes and lakes

Further information

Books to read

A *Flavour of China* by Amy Shui and Stuart Thompson (Wayland, 2006)

Country Insights: China by Julia Waterlow (Wayland, 2006)

Kids Around the World Celebrate!: The Best Feasts and Festivals from Many Lands by Lynda Jones (John Wiley & Sons, 2000)

Let's Eat! What Children Eat Around the World by Beatrice Hollyer (Frances Lincoln, 2003)

We Come from China by Julia Waterlow (Wayland, 2002)

A World of Recipes: China by Julie McCulloch (Heinemann, 2001)

Websites

CIA Factbook

www.cia.gov/cia/publications/factbook

Facts and figures about China and other countries.

Chinatown Online

www.chinatown-online.co.uk

Information about Chinese food and culture with activities for children.

About.com

http://chinesefood.about.com

Information and recipes for Chinese dishes.

Index

All the numbers in **bold** refer to photographs as well as text.